ARCTIC

DISCOVERIES

Images from Voyages of
Four Decades in the North

JOHN R. BOCKSTOCE

The History Bank
in association with
University of Washington Press • Seattle and London

© 2000 John R. Bockstoce

Published in the United States of America by the University of Washington Press, PO Box 50096, Seattle, WA 98145-5096, and in Canada by McGill-Queen's University Press, 3430 McTavish Street, Montreal, Quebec, Canada H3A 1X9

Library of Congress Cataloging-in-Publication Data

Bockstoce, John R.
    Arctic discoveries : images from voyages of four decades in the North / John R. Bockstoce.
      p. cm.
    ISBN 0-295-98015-X
     1. Arctic regions--Description and travel. 2. Arctic regions--Pictorial works. 3. Bockstoce, John R.--Journeys--Arctic regions. I. History Bank (Firm) II. Title.

    G608 .B63 2000
    919.804--dc21

                                      00-030236

Book development and coordination for the University of Washington Press by The History Bank Inc., Woodinville, Washington.

Project coordination   Laura Fisher
Design and layout   Sandra J. Harner
Original map art   Kelly C. Rush

Printed in Canada by Quality Color Press, Edmonton, Alberta

Other Books by John R. Bockstoce

The Eskimos of Northwest Alaska in the Early Nineteenth Century (1977)

Steam Whaling in the Western Arctic (1977)

The Archaeology of Cape Nome, Alaska (1979)

American Whalers in the Western Arctic (1986) (With William Gilkerson)

Whales, Ice and Men: The History of Commercial Whaling in the Western Arctic (1986)

Arctic Passages: A Unique Small-Boat Journey Through the Great Northern Waterway (1991)

The Voyage of the Schooner Polar Bear: Whaling and Trading in the North Pacific and Arctic, 1913–1914, from the Journal of Bernhard Killian (1983). Edited by John R. Bockstoce.

The Journal of Rochfort Maguire, 1852–1854: Two Years at Point Barrow, Alaska Aboard HMS Plover *in the Search for Sir John Franklin* (1988). Edited by John R. Bockstoce.

ARCTIC

DISCOVERIES

Images from Voyages of
Four Decades in the North

for

Bonnie Hahn

Contents

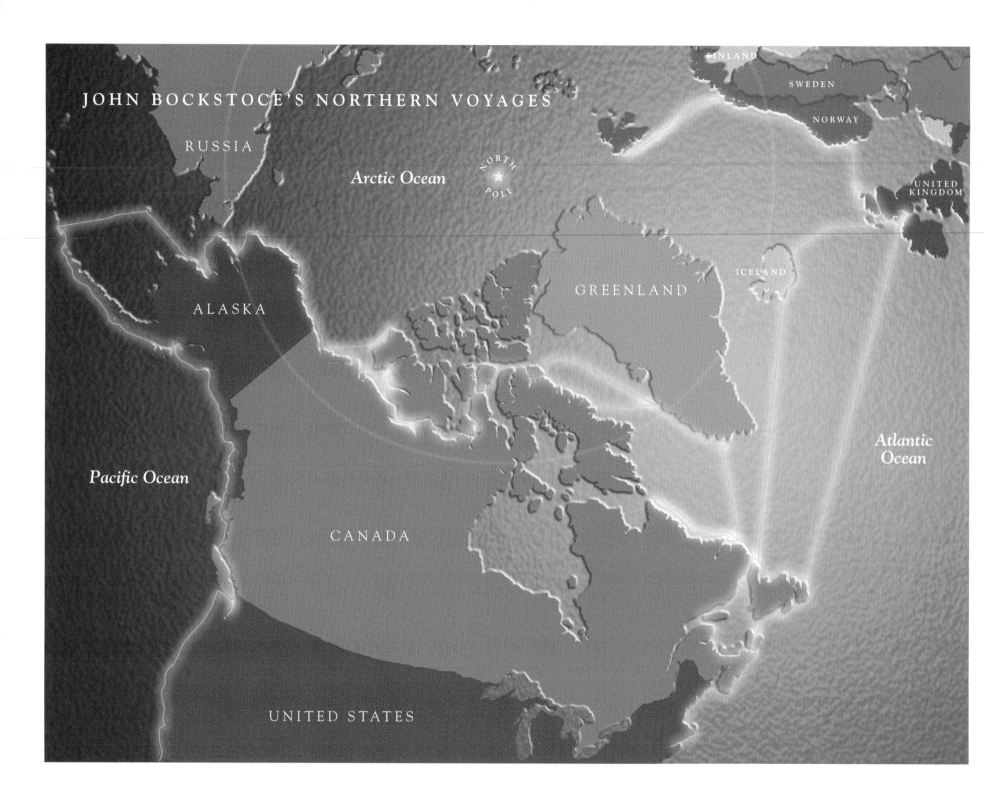

JOHN BOCKSTOCE'S NORTHERN VOYAGES

RUSSIA

Arctic Ocean

NORTH
POLE

FINLAND

SWEDEN

NORWAY

UNITED
KINGDOM

ALASKA

GREENLAND

ICELAND

Pacific Ocean

Atlantic
Ocean

CANADA

UNITED STATES

Introduction

THE AIR WAS PERFECTLY CLEAR one evening in June 1971, on the shore of the Arctic Ocean. I was on the gravel beach of the Point Hope Peninsula, the low, wave-formed spit that juts twenty-five miles into the Chukchi Sea from mainland Alaska. More than one hundred miles north of the Arctic Circle, it wasn't dark at all there, but the light had an almost velvet quality, as the sun— deep orange against a purple sky—stood low on the northern horizon.

To the east it softly washed the fifty-mile palisade of cliffs and headlands, highlighting the deep ravines and gorges of what is the last vestige of the Rocky Mountains, the northern terminus of the cordillera that begins in Tierra del Fuego, at the southern tip of South America. Here they finally plunge into the sea. It is this massive bulwark that forces offshore the ocean current that flows north from the Pacific Ocean through Bering Strait, creating in its lee a placid gyre that drops its water-borne sediment. Over many millennia, autumn storms have heaped this debris into beach ridges, forming the long, curving Point Hope Peninsula that the Eskimos call *Tikigaq*, "index finger."

I was about six miles east of the tip of the index finger that evening. I remember the softest of southeasterly breezes blowing, barely noticeable, and so light that it hardly rippled the surface of the dark sea—a darkness that was made deeper by the brilliance of the white ice floes dappling the water as they marched westward, carried by the ocean current in silent procession.

I was camped there with an Eskimo family. Six or seven of us were on the beach. Nothing much was happening, but we felt the fine, cool air brushing our faces as we drank coffee, each lost in his or her thoughts while we worked on repairs, sewing and other small chores. We were all glad to be outdoors at last and away from the winter confines of small houses in town and the exhaustion and sometimes searing cold of ice-edge whaling camps in April and May. Now, in mid-June, the Chukchi Sea's thick winter ice covering had broken up and was melting fast as it flowed north. Boat travel had begun, and many families had returned to the land, to their summer campsites, to savor the freedom of the short summer.

Songbirds fluttered among the wildflowers and beach grasses behind us, where several large sealskins were pegged out, hair-down, drying in the summer's warmth. In front of our two white canvas wall tents, our sealskin-covered umiak—a light, durable boat shaped like a Grand Banks dory—was drawn up on the beach, and beside me one or two men sat quietly scanning the water with their rifles resting easily across their outstretched legs. Even though the whaling season, with all its hardship and reward, was past, these men had to prepare for the next season's hunt. Sealskins were a necessity for their boots and boat covers, to say nothing of their need for the quantities of rich meat and oil these animals provided.

Every now and then the sound of a faint splash near shore would pop them into high alert. Was it a piece of ice falling from the edge of one of the melting floes—or was it a seal surfacing for air? If someone spotted a glossy, black seal's head, a rifle would snap up and just as quickly the crack of a shot would ring out. If successful, we would run to the boat and launch it quickly to get to the seal before it sank. If we were lucky we would pull the carcass aboard with a boat hook, but if it was below the surface, we would have to lower a four-pronged retrieving hook and try to snag it to bring it up.

Once ashore, we hauled the carcass up the beach, where one or two women with razor-sharp crescent-shaped knives, "*ulus*," bent over the seal and began skinning it. Meanwhile, the children roamed over the beaches, slept in the tent, or helped their parents. Just inside one of the tent flaps a gasoline pressure stove would be heating water to make seal stew. Soon its rich aroma would call us to dinner.

For me, such moments were the most wonderful part of the Arctic year: the weather was usually good, the light was constant, the living was easy, and time seemed to stand still. Without the abrupt caesura of day and night, we slept when we wanted, got up when we were ready, and enjoyed the summer days. I usually joined in the hunt or camp work or accompanied an expedition in the umiak to the bird cliffs at Cape Thompson, twenty miles to the southeast. There, hundreds of thousands of murres (guillemot-like birds) and other sea birds migrate to lay their eggs in the protection of the cliffs. Feeding in the rich waters below, so many birds were diving from the cliffs, swooping about, splashing into the water, and returning to their perches that it seemed as if we were amidst a huge swarm of bees.

We would gather as many eggs as we could from the lower cliff faces, place them gently in the umiak, then shoot a few murres and cook them in a driftwood fire on the beach. After a couple of hours' nap we would head back to our camp with the eggs. It never mattered what time it was, and in fact, I frequently lost track of time during those days and nights.

That evening in 1971, I walked back from our camp to the foot of a long, low hill where I wandered among the faint mounds of sod that marked the perimeters of houses, the remains of a peculiar village called Jabbertown. As an archaeologist, I was interested in ruins, but it was easy to see that these were not the remains of traditional Inupiaq (Eskimo) houses. Their shapes betrayed them as being foreign. In fact, this village had only sprung up in the 1880s, during the heyday of commercial whaling, when the price of whalebone (baleen) was sky-high.

Here, a polyglot immigrant community of Eskimos, Irish, Germans, Black and White Americans, Portuguese, and other nationalities came together at a prime spot to hunt the bowhead whales, somewhat in the Eskimo fashion: not from pelagic whaleships, but from small boats in the leads in the pack ice during the spring. At only a few places in Alaska does the bowheads' migration pass close to shore, but the Point Hope Peninsula's long thrust into the ocean is one of those spots. Thus, commercial whalemen were drawn there, and for a short time a couple of dozen makeshift houses sheltered them.

Nevertheless, by the first years of the twentieth century this relentless pursuit had forced the whales close to extinction, and then the changing whims of fashion collapsed the baleen market. Narrow-waisted corsets were no longer in vogue; hence baleen was no longer required for corset stays. Just as quickly as they had congregated at Jabbertown, the whalemen drifted away.

In June 1971 I was only in my third summer in Alaska. But my interest in the North had begun ten years before, in the summer after my graduation from high school, when I took a job as a volunteer laborer for a medical mission in Newfoundland and Labrador. As I wrote in my book *Arctic Passages*, on arrival in Flowers Cove, Newfoundland, "I fell in love with the area . . . in the heady thrill of being on my own in a remote region. It was incredibly exciting to gaze across the Strait of Belle Isle at the Labrador coast, low and blue in the morning haze. With the voyages of the first European discoverers fresh in my mind, it seemed a heroic place. It wasn't very far north, but it felt like a frontier, and I was as happy as if I had been standing on the northern tip of Greenland. That day . . . the North reached out and grabbed me, and to this day, I am glad to say, it has never released its grip."

At that moment I was indeed fortunate to discover in myself a strong desire to be in the North and to learn as much about it as I could. Driven by this fascination, in college I majored in anthropology, with a specialization in Canadian Inuits, and later, on my way to a doctorate in arctic archaeology, I shifted my attention to the western Arctic and began a series of excavations near

Bering Strait in Alaska. Because there was a whaling element to the prehistoric sites that I was investigating, I wanted to learn more about this difficult and rewarding pursuit, so in 1971 I began a ten-year hitch, serving each spring as a member of a whaling crew at Point Hope.

The experience of Eskimo whaling led me in turn to a curiosity about how the historical American whaling industry and the maritime fur trade had contributed to change in the Arctic in the nineteenth and early twentieth centuries. To probe the subject further, throughout the 1970s I used an Eskimo walrus-hide umiak to travel along the shore of Arctic North America in search of shipwrecks, graves, and abandoned settlements from that era.

I traveled 6,000 miles in the umiak (it is now in Connecticut, part of Mystic Seaport Museum's collections), but when I needed to work farther offshore, to visit distant islands, I bought a sturdy steel-hulled, long-range motor-sailer to expand the research. These voyages continued throughout the 1980s. I left my boat, *Belvedere*, in advanced bases: for five winters near the mouth of the Mackenzie River in western Arctic Canada and another on the west coast of Greenland. I reached New England in 1989, incidentally having completed the first eastbound yacht traverse of the Northwest Passage. My book *Arctic Passages* describes those voyages.

But the call of the North was still strong. I immediately began a thorough refit of *Belvedere* to allow me to explore further, this time in the North Atlantic. In 1991, with a crew of six, I crossed the Atlantic from New England, via Newfoundland, to Scotland. The next year we sailed to nearly 80 degrees north latitude (less than 700 miles from the North Pole) on the coast of Spitsbergen.

I returned to North America in 1993, along a Viking route: the Outer Hebrides, Faeroe Islands, Iceland and Newfoundland. Since then, with the exception of another Northwest Passage traverse aboard a friend's boat in 1994, I have been sailing on the coast of Labrador. My feelings for the North continue to be remarkably similar to those I experienced at Jabbertown.

That evening I had climbed the hill behind the abandoned settlement and gazed south over our campsite and out over the ocean. Then I turned to the east, my eyes following the line of cliffs and hills from Cape Thompson to Cape Lisburne. I remember very well how happy and full of peace I felt, for all the things that I love about the North were at hand: the solitude; the beauty of the land, sky, water, and ice; the people and their livelihood; and the littered remains of the Arctic's history.

Today as I look through the thousands and thousands of photographs that I have taken since 1962, I find that the images fall into the same broad themes that struck me that evening in 1971. Accordingly, I have arranged them in this book primarily in chronological groups, encompassing my early work in Alaska and the North Pacific, later in the Canadian Arctic, and, most recently, in the North Atlantic.

Arctic Ocean

Beaufort Sea

Chukchi Sea

ICY REEF

BROOKS RANGE

CAPE LISBURNE

RUSSIA

POINT HOPE ○ ○ CAPE THOMPSON

○ ANAKTUVUK PASS

ARCTIC CIRCLE

Bering Strait

Yukon River

Diomede ○ ○ CAPE PRINCE OF WALES
Islands

Seward Peninsula

ALASKA

CANADA

PORT CLARENCE
○

SAFETY
LAGOON ○

St. Lawrence
Island

○ ST. MICHAEL

○ RUSSIAN MISSION

St. Matthew
Island

INTERNATIONAL DATE LINE

Bering Sea

Alaska Peninsula

Aleutian Islands

IKATAN
BAY ○

Pacific Ocean

North Pacific and Western Arctic

I FIRST VISITED THE WESTERN ARCTIC in 1969 with a Swiss archaeological expedition to Saint Lawrence Island, Alaska, near Bering Strait. I immediately was absorbed by the complicated ecology and human history of this region, where two continents and two oceans come together, and strong currents from the North Pacific provide nutrients to the waters from which the inhabitants draw their livelihood.

Back on mainland Alaska later that summer, I came upon an interesting archaeological site on the beach ridges near Cape Nome on the south coast of the Seward Peninsula. I returned there in the following years to carry out a series of excavations. At almost the same time, I began my decade of membership, each spring, with an Eskimo whaling crew at Point Hope. I expanded my knowledge of the region in 1977 during a canoe descent of the lower Yukon River and coastal voyage on Norton Sound. In 1983, when I returned to the western Arctic aboard *Belvedere*, I paralleled the Alaska Peninsula before turning north to traverse the Bering, Chukchi, and Beaufort seas.

Aleutian Islands and Bering Sea

Alaska Peninsula

Ikatan Bay, False Pass, Alaska

There is a wild beauty to these bold coasts, which are the jagged remains of volcanic calderae. For the mariner, however, they pose a dual danger: undersea spines of rock are a hazard, and in protected bays the bottom may be too deep to anchor.

Belvedere found shelter in Ikatan Bay at the mouth of False Pass, the easternmost (and very shallow) water passage between the Pacific Ocean and Bering Sea. My son, Johnny, inspected an eagle's nest from above.

Saint Matthew Island, Bering Sea

Halfway between the Aleutian Islands and Bering Strait—and almost equidistant between Asia and America—Saint Matthew Island is one of the least accessible places in the Northern Hemisphere, lacking as it does a safe anchorage or suitable terrain for an airstrip. Uninhabited, and rarely visited by human beings, its steep cliffs are the summer home of millions of seabirds.

Here, a lone crew member walks through the northern mists across the lush, rolling tundra, amid the cries of seabirds.

Russian Mission

In June 1977 I took a twenty-foot freighter canoe 1,400 miles down the Tanana and Yukon rivers and along the coast of the Bering Sea, from Fairbanks to Nome, Alaska. One evening on the lower Yukon, just as the light was fading, we reached the settlement of Russian Mission, a village of 200 Eskimos that was dominated, on a bluff above, by a tin-roofed Russian Orthodox church that supported Russian crosses on its ridge poles.

The next morning was sunny and calm, and few people were stirring in the town. In the silence I walked up to the church, and through the dusty glass window I saw a priest, accompanied only by an acolyte, saying Mass in full ecclesiastical vestments. I could feel the warm, comforting hand of Mother Russia reaching out from more than a century before.

Yukon River Sternwheelers

When gold was discovered in the Klondike in 1896, and the gold rush began in 1898, the Yukon River immediately took on a new importance as a way of transporting heavy freight 1,600 miles from the ocean to the goldfields. Ships carried cargo to Saint Michael, Alaska, near the mouth of the river, then transferred it to the Yukon sternwheelers. It took fifteen days or more to reach the town of Dawson in the Yukon Territory. Bucking the current, the steamers used prodigious amounts of firewood—up to two cords per hour. Because they needed to take on wood as often as twice a day, woodcutters set up camps every thirty miles or so along the river. Hundreds of men were employed cutting firewood and stacking it at the river's edge.

However, traffic on the Saint Michael route immediately fell off when a railroad was built, from Alaska's Pacific Ocean ports to Nenana, on the Tanana River. The last boats were beached in 1942, and the remaining freight was moved by diesel tugs and barges. When the boats were laid up, they themselves were rapidly scavenged for firewood.

In a marsh near St. Michael in 1977, I came upon these ghostly reminders of another era.

Bering Strait Region

Saint Lawrence Island

In 1969 in the village of Gambell, on Saint Lawrence Island, I met the famous artist Florence Malewotkuk, who held her grandson in pride. I admired the delicate lines on her hands and face: She had come of age in a very different world and had been tattooed in the traditional manner of the Saint Lawrence Islanders.

Later, I stayed briefly at the Irrigoo family's hunting camp, where the head of the family, Samuel Irrigoo, steered his walrus-hide umiak to retrieve a seal that his son had just shot from shore.

Bering Strait

Cape Prince of Wales, Alaska, is the western tip of continental North America. Standing amid the sand dunes in the little Eskimo village in 1969, I looked out across Bering Strait. It was a dramatic scene: Shafts of light broke through the low clouds, Fairway Rock stood out clearly, and in the distance, halfway to the eastern tip of Asia, Little Diomede was bracketed by Big Diomede.

A day or two later I climbed the steep slope of the Cape itself to visit an old graveyard. There I found the remains of an Eskimo whaling captain who, in the traditional manner, had been laid to rest with his prized hunting implements. But the outside world's intrusion was evident, too—a small cross was fixed to the wooden box, above his head.

Several times I have traveled there by boat, during the great springtime migration of the walrus herds. A quarter of a million walruses ride the retreating ice floes through Bering Strait into the Arctic Ocean, feeding on the rich clam beds in those shallow waters and sleeping piled atop one another on the ice.

One day, when we were very close to the International Date Line, we came upon a small group of walruses, while behind them Big Diomede Island, then part of the U.S.S.R., formed a cold backdrop. Later that day—and a few miles to the north—with Little Diomede on the left and Big Diomede on the right, I realized that within my view were two of everything: two continents (North America and Asia), two oceans (the Pacific and the Arctic), two seas (the Bering and the Chukchi), two nations (the U.S.A. and the U.S.S.R.), and two days (today and tomorrow).

Safety Lagoon, Seward Peninsula

I began my archaeological excavations on the Seward Peninsula, investigating an ancient village on the beach ridges east of Cape Nome. It was a beautiful, quiet spot, where across the waters of Safety Lagoon were the foothills of the Kigluaik Mountains.

TEN.

Port Clarence, Seward Peninsula

Port Clarence, the great bay fifty miles southeast of Bering Strait, is formed by the curving arm of Cape Spencer's gravel spit. This excellent harbor first came to the attention of Europeans in 1826, when Captain Frederick William Beechey of Britain's Royal Navy charted it. Since then it has sheltered the nineteenth-century whaling fleets and a gaggle of Gold Rush vessels in the early years of the twentieth century. Most recently it has served as a haven for the tug and barge fleets heading to the North Slope oil fields.

Early in August 1983, en route from Seattle to the Beaufort Sea aboard *Belvedere*, we entered Port Clarence just as a gale was clearing. The silhouette of the massive barges and their cargoes stood out against a moody evening sky.

Point Hope

ॐ

Point Hope

Captain James Cook's voyage north of Bering Strait in 1778 produced the first accurate delineation of the northern coasts of Alaska, but because Cook prudently kept his ships some distance from shore, he did not discover Port Clarence, Kotzebue Sound or Point Hope. Russian explorers charted Kotzebue Sound and Point Hope early in the nineteenth century, but it remained for Frederick William Beechey to complete the surveys as far as Point Barrow, the northernmost point of Alaska. On August 2, 1826, when Beechey's men climbed to the top of Cape Thompson, they were astonished to see the great curving arc of the Point Hope Peninsula. Because of the authority and worldwide dissemination of British charts in the nineteenth century, Beechey's choice for the peninsula's name has survived, replacing an earlier Russian name, Cape Golovnin. In my first view of the peninsula, I understood how Beechey's crew must have felt.

Whaling Crew Waiting at the Ice Edge

In April and May, when the Arctic Ocean's ice cover begins to break up, bowhead whales swim north from the Bering Sea and through the Chukchi Sea to their summer feeding grounds in the Beaufort Sea. For a thousand years, the Eskimos of northern Alaska have hunted these great creatures. The whales' meat and blubber form a major part of the Eskimos' winter food supply.

The hunt goes on round the clock, but most of it requires waiting patiently, alertly and quietly at the ice edge, sometimes in severe cold. One or two men always scan the horizon for a bowhead's v-shaped blow, while nearby the sealskin-covered umiak is ready to launch, with a harpoon and two darting guns projecting over the bow.

The darting guns and the heavy 28-pound bronze shoulder gun (here held by my friend Ungsi Long, who is also shown steering an umiak) are nineteenth-century Yankee inventions that fire small time-delay bombs and hasten the whale's death.

In the lulls between the bowheads' runs, the Eskimos seek other game: seals, ducks and beluga whales. On the ice beside the whaleboat are rifles and shotguns and a light retrieving harpoon.

Chasing a Bowhead

One calm day in May 1976, a whaling crew paddled quietly past me, down the water lead between the shore-fast ice and the moving pack ice. The traditional Eskimo umiak is a vessel of marvelous simplicity and durability. It is made of sealskins sewn together and stretched over a driftwood frame, which itself is lashed at the joints, not rigidly fastened. Its lightness, tough hide covering, and flexible frame make it an ideal boat for work among the ice floes.

Preparing to Tow a Whale Ashore

Exhausted, Point Hope's whaling crews take advantage of an exceptionally calm and warm day to rest after a successful four-hour pursuit, with the whale, supine, before them. After reciting the Lord's Prayer in thanks, they will begin the bone-tiring job of towing the carcass several miles to the nearest shore-fast ice.

Coffee Break on the Chukchi Sea

After towing two whales
to the edge of the shore-
fast ice, the crews of eight
whaleboats have worked
for three hours with a
massive block-and-tackle to
haul the forty-ton carcass
up onto the ice. In 1976,
we took a brief break
before the twelve-hour job
of butchering the whale
began. My friend Norman
Omnik enjoyed his coffee
in the whale's lee.

Butchering Bowhead Whales

One crew's success is shared by the entire community. First the skin and blubber are stripped from the carcass, then the meat is cut away, and finally the bones and entrails are taken. The food is stored frozen, year-round, in deep cellars dug into the permafrost.

After butchering the whale, the hunters at Point Hope return the whale's massive skull to the ocean, believing that the spirit of the whale lives within the skull, and if it is thus treated honorably, it will return to reward them with other captures.

When the butchering is done, all that will remain is a large patch of blood-soaked ice and a small pile of useless entrails, upon which the gulls will feed for days.

On the Chuckchi Sea, May 1977

The experience of participating in the Eskimos' whale hunt contributed to my book *Whales, Ice and Men*. Here I am shouldering a bomb lance gun. In the background are the foothills north of Cape Thompson.

Anaktuvuk Pass, 1970

Living in the mountainous divide between the Arctic Slope and the Yukon drainage, the inhabitants of Anaktuvuk Pass are the descendants of a group of Inupiaq (Eskimos) who have historically had little contact with the ocean. Their lives have been focused on the vast herds of caribou that migrate annually through the passes of the Brooks Range, moving north and south between their winter range and their calving grounds on the Arctic coast.

So regular have been the caribou migrations through the pass that "Anaktuvuk" in Inupiaq means "place of caribou dung."

Weather Front in the Beaufort Sea

In August 1994, I made another traverse of the Northwest Passage, this time aboard a friend's boat. Just as we were off Icy Reef, near the Alaska-Yukon border, a storm front swept down on us from the mountains of Alaska's Brooks Range. When the front reached us, the wind suddenly came up out of the northwest in force, while the temperature dropped twenty degrees.

GREENLAND

**Ellesmere
Island**

Otto Fiord

Arctic Ocean

Baffin Bay

**Beaufort
Sea**

CAPE PRINCE
ALFRED ○   *McClure Strait*

Cornwallis
Island   *Lancaster Sound*

RESOLUTE BAY ○   Barrow Strait   Bylot
Island

**Banks
Island**   PRINCE   ● CAPE
                            LEOPOLD   CRAUFORD
                            ISLAND ●

Herschel ○
Island   **Baffin Island**

DUCK HAWK ○
BLUFF

Firth River

DE SALIS ○
NELSON BAY
HEAD ○   ○ WALKER BAY

Bathurst
Peninsula   **Victoria
                                                Island**   Boothia
                                                Peninsula   ● IGLOOLIK

YUKON   BALAENA ○   *Amundsen Gulf*   *Larsen
              BAY   Sound*

SMOKING HILLS ○   *James Ross Strait*

              PEARCE POINT
              ○ HARBOUR   King
                                                        William
                                        Dolphin & Union Strait Island

Horton River

              BERNARD ○
              HARBOUR   *Queen Maud Gulf*

Parry Peninsula

Coronation Gulf *Bathurst Inlet*

ARCTIC CIRCLE

Canadian Arctic

My first visit to the Canadian Arctic was in 1965, when I worked as a laborer for a small air service in the settlement of Resolute on Cornwallis Island. Five years later I flew to the village of Igloolik as an assistant to an NBC News documentary crew, but in 1972 I entered the Arctic Canada from the west, via the Beaufort Sea, on the first of my umiak voyages. I spent much of the next twenty summers in Canada's northern waters, probing farther and farther east in various parts of the Northwest Passage, first with the umiak and later with my motor-sailer, *Belvedere.*

Valley of the Firth River

Close to the Alaska-Yukon boundary the Firth River flows north, out of the Richardson Mountains into the Beaufort Sea. In the center of the river's outwash plain is a small, bold bluff called "Engigstciak." For four thousand years hunters have used Engigstciak for spotting the herds of caribou that migrate along the Arctic coastal plain.

Eskimo Graves, Herschel Island, Yukon Territory

The bleaching headboards on Herschel Island's flower-covered and grassy hills recall a nearly forgotten era of Arctic history. Herschel Island is now deserted, save for one family that summers there, but in the last years of the nineteenth century it was a community of a thousand whalemen and Eskimos. The Yankee whalemen began using Herschel Island's harbor in 1889 as they pursued the bowhead whales into their last refuge in the eastern Beaufort Sea. As many as fifteen ships wintered there each year, waiting ten months for the ice to retreat and the brief whaling season to begin.

Herschel Island was the only place on the coast of western Arctic Canada where manufactured goods were available. Many Eskimos from Canada's Mackenzie River delta and Alaska's Brooks Range took up residence as hunters, supplying the ships with fresh meat.

After the collapse of the whaling industry in 1908, a few natives remained because the Hudson's Bay Company set up a trading post there, and several maritime traders used Herschel's harbor as an Arctic outpost.

The Horton River and the Smoking Hills

The meandering Horton River breaks through the 300-foot mud cliffs of the Bathurst Peninsula and debouches into Franklin Bay, where it has created a low delta that has been the home of trappers and traders. I found the site littered with a few wooden barrel stays and five generations of metal barrels—the legacy of the whaling industry and the fur trade. Bears had broken in the cabins' windows.

Nearby are the famous Smoking Hills. Although Europeans only came upon them in 1826, the hills may have been burning for thousands of years. Amid the eroding mud banks, microscopic pyrite spontaneously combusts upon exposure to oxygen and ignites the bituminous shale nearby. The acrid smoke has a raw, sulphurous odor.

Recently, scientists have been studying the surrounding vegetation to determine species of plants that might survive in similarly polluted industrial environments.

Cape Parry's Whaling Remains

The Parry Peninsula juts fifty miles north from the mainland into Amundsen Gulf. In contrast to the greenery and high hills on the west side of Franklin Bay, the peninsula's crumbling limestone cliffs are a uniform raw ochre. There we came upon the remains of the steam whaling bark *Alexander*.

On August 13, 1906, she was charging along in a dense fog under both sail and steam. At 7:00 A.M., just as the officers were sitting down to breakfast, the ship struck hard on Cape Parry. They abandoned her almost at once, the crew sailing five hundred miles in their whaleboats to rescue at Herschel Island. The derelict was, of course, a godsend for the local trappers, both white and Eskimo, for whom it was a wonderful source of supplies and raw materials.

Rounding one of the low, limestone outcroppings, I spotted a massive rusty iron boiler lying against the foot of the cliff. It was all that remained of the

Alexander. Nearby, on a barren hillside, stood two grave markers. These were not from the *Alexander* disaster, but rather ten years earlier, when the whaleships *Balaena* and *Grampus* had cruised too late in the autumn in Amundsen Gulf. Heavy ice blocked their way back to Herschel Island, and with no other recourse, the ships were forced to spend the long winter of 1895–1896 in Balaena Bay at Cape Parry. They were very short of rations and, thus weakened, eight men died.

Both headboards were carved from heavy wooden planks that were now gray and weather-beaten. They hinted to the New England origins of their makers: One had a low and rounded top, like a seventeenth-century gravestone; the other was seven and a half feet tall and shaped like an eighteenth-century church spire, and perched at its apex was a lovely carved dove of peace.

Along the edges were a number of puncture marks, evidence that bears had recently been gnawing on the boards. A few tufts of fluffy brown hair were stuck on the splinters as well—a grizzly bear had used the marker as a scratching post.

On the graves themselves were little clumps of wildflowers. I remember how silent and lonely it was.

Natural Bridge, Pearce Point Harbour

Across Darnley Bay from Cape Parry, the limestone cliffs continue, and Pearce Point Harbour is the last haven on the continental coast for two hundred miles. In the center of the harbor a layer-cake limestone island forms a handsome natural bridge. We tried to go through it in the dinghy, but the force of the wind funneling through the hole lifted our little dinghy right out of the water. We decided to pass on that idea.

In 1986 and 1987 I cruised on the north coast of Amundsen Gulf searching for remains of the whaling industry and the fur trade.

Nelson Head, Banks Island

Rising from the sea to more than 2,400 feet, Nelson Head, at the southernmost point of Banks Island, is one of western Arctic Canada's great natural wonders. In 1850, during the search for Sir John Franklin's missing Arctic expedition, Robert McClure, commanding the H.M.S. *Investigator*, was the first European to see these proterozoic limestone and dolomite cliffs. He named the cliffs after Britain's naval hero of the Napoleonic Wars, Admiral Lord Nelson. Very early one morning, as we rounded the cape, fog began billowing over the tops.

Cape Prince Alfred, Banks Island

I followed the *Investigator's* route up the west coast of Banks Island. At the northwest corner of the island, Cape Prince Alfred, we turned east into McClure Strait, waters where few vessels have ever been. The fog and ice were very close there, and it reminded me of the price that McClure had paid for his temerity: The ice caught his ship and held it for more than two years. McClure was forced to abandon the *Investigator* and walk to the safety of rescue ships in the eastern Arctic. He and his crew thereby became the first men to traverse a northwest passage, albeit partially on foot.

After a brief reconnaissance in the strait, I turned *Belvedere's* bow back toward the south and the comparative safety of Amundsen Gulf.

Duck Hawk Bluff, Banks Island

After a night crossing of Amundsen Gulf, we anchored off Duck Hawk Bluff with a dramatic sunrise.

De Salis Bay, Banks Island

The mud in the low hills behind De Salis Bay has been forced into web-like patterns by the freezing and thawing of the groundwater. Small plants grow in the cracks, sheltered there from the wind.

St. Roch's Cairn, Walker Bay, Victoria Island

The few visitors to Walker Bay have been struck by the raw beauty of its limestone cliffs. For sailors, however, its attraction has been shelter from moving sea ice.

The first Europeans to winter here were Captain Richard Collinson and the crew of H.M.S. *Enterprise* (1851–1852), during the search for Sir John Franklin's missing expedition. Almost ninety years later Sergeant Henry Larsen of the Royal Canadian Mounted Police put *St. Roch* in winter quarters here during the second traverse of the Northwest Passage. His crew built the cairn.

Inner Northwest Passage

I have spent parts of six summers in what could be called the "inner northwest passage"—the waters between Dolphin and Union Strait in the west and Lancaster Sound in the east. Because these waterways are relatively narrow, big seas are not as much of a problem as is the sea ice, which melts slowly in those constricted waters.

Bernard Harbour

In the first years of the twentieth century, Captain Joseph Bernard wintered in the shelter of Bernard Harbour during one of his pioneering fur trading voyages. The harbor later was used as a base for the Canadian Arctic Expedition, and soon the Hudson's Bay Company and Anglican Church established themselves there as well.

The northern approach to the harbor is difficult to spot, and this rough-and-ready, but effective, early navigational marker—two barrels of different ages—still remains. Curiously enough, it is also a good radar target for today's navigators.

In the 1930s the Hudson's Bay Company experimented with snow tractors—Ford V-Eight Snowfliers. The skeleton of one remains next to the old trading post.

Dolphin and Union Strait

Sea ice of only one winter's age is rarely thicker than seven feet and usually melts away during the summer. If, however, it survives into a second winter, it will have lost most of its salt and become harder and denser, making it a greater hazard to navigation.

Here, *Belvedere* forces her way through rotten first-year ice on her way into Coronation Gulf.

Bathurst Inlet

Running south 150 miles from Coronation Gulf to the Arctic Circle, Bathurst Inlet is a long cleft in the precambrian rocks of the great geological formation called the Canadian Shield. One of the granite outcrops on the east side of the Inlet provided a good anchorage for *Belvedere*. In the distance is the mouth of the Burnside River.

Taking on Fresh Water in Queen Maud Gulf

Sea ice that is more than one winter old has lost most of its salt and therefore can be used for drinking water. Cruising through the pack ice, we kept a lookout for a large old floe that had a melt water pond on it. If the pond was far enough away from the edge of the floe, and hence not contaminated by salt spray, it was a simple matter to put our emergency bilge pump on the ice and fill the water tanks through a garden hose.

James Ross Strait

There are as many as eight different water routes through the Northwest Passage. For smaller vessels, however, the only practical one is via James Ross Strait, the narrow waterway separating King William Island from the Boothia Peninsula.

In September 1987 we found heavy, closely packed ice stretching across the strait from shore to shore, forcing us to return a thousand miles to our wintering harbor near the Mackenzie River delta.

We tried again in 1988, and although the ice brought us to a halt in the same place, the conditions seemed more favorable than the previous year. Waiting for an opening, we anchored in an unnamed harbor on the Boothia Peninsula shore, while my son, Johnny, then twelve years old, used the time to practice some ice navigation of his own in very shallow water. The floes soon parted, allowing us to move on to Greenland and thus to complete the first eastbound yacht traverse of the Northwest Passage.

I returned there six years later aboard the converted former oil rig supply vessel, *Itasca*. The ice again blocked our progress in exactly the same spot, but we were fortunate: The Canadian Coast Guard icebreaker *Sir John Franklin* offered to escort us through the pack ice. One evening, with a spooky mist rising, she suddenly loomed out of the murk, bright red and more than 300 feet long.

The next morning she set off at eight knots through the ice. We immediately felt the floes crashing against the hull as we left the strait and charged north, into Larsen Sound.

Otto Fiord, Ellesmere Island

I flew to Otto Fiord, an embayment of the Arctic Ocean on northern Ellesmere Island. The fiord was choked with ice, and it seemed that the icebergs that had calved from its glacier had hardly moved in years.

Resolute Bay

In 1965 I found a summer job in the town of Resolute on Cornwallis Island, at the western end of Barrow Strait. One evening in July, as I walked over the ice on the still-frozen harbor, I saw a faint speck to seaward, an Inuk (Eskimo) with his dog team, returning to the village from seal hunting.

Prince Leopold Island

Twenty-nine years after my first view of Barrow Strait (from Cornwallis Island) I transited its south shore, aboard *Itasca*. Working through loosely packed ice along the coast of Somerset Island, the fog lifted as we approached its northeastern corner, revealing the thousand-foot, flat topped Prince Leopold Island amid the drifting floes. It reminded me that we had truly reached the eastern Arctic: In the nineteenth century this island was a prominent landmark for the whalemen and explorers who sailed here from Great Britain.

Approaching Cape Crauford, Baffin Island

In a helicopter from *Itasca*, I flew over the sere, dun-colored sedimentary cliffs near the northernmost point of Baffin Island.

Glacier, Bylot Island

An icebreaker captain said to me many years ago, "Ice is just hard water," a point that was driven home to me when I saw the ductility of a glacier's flow on Bylot Island, off northern Baffin Island.

Igloolik

I worked with an NBC News documentary team in the winter of 1970 in the settlement of Igloolik, in northern Foxe Basin. We flew there in a Douglas DC-3 aircraft and landed on the ice of the bay. Later we accompanied a young Inuk hunter, Jean Baptiste Illupalik, to hunt for seals. His caribou-hide clothing gave him perfect protection from the penetrating sub-zero cold. Hugh Downs and I chose to sleep in an igloo rather than a heated house. The glow from a seal-oil lamp, tended by Rosie Iqalliyuk Okkumaluk, gave a beautiful, soft light.

Labrador

- CAPE WHITE HANDKERCHIEF
- RAMAH
- BEAR'S GUT
- HEBRON
- BISHOP'S MITRE
- MAN O'WAR BROOK
- NAIN
- INSIDE PASSAGE
- HOPEDALE
- WEST TURNAVIK ISLAND
- MAKKOVIK
- CAPE HARRISON
- PORCUPINE STRAND
- INDIAN TICKLE
- PENNEY HARBOUR
- HAWKE HARBOUR
- BATTLE HARBOUR
- CHATEAU BAY
- RED BAY
- *Strait of Belle Isle*

SVALBARD

Barents Sea

AMSTERDAMØYA
DANSKØYA
Spitsbergen

BELLSUND

HORNSUND

Greenland Sea

Baffin Island

GREENLAND

ARCTIC CIRCLE

Norwegian Sea

ICELAND

NORWAY

FAERINGSHAVN

Labrador

CANADA

Labrador Sea

ARSUK FIORD

Labrador Sea

Faeroe Islands

Shetland Islands

SCOTLAND

LOCH TARBERT

Atlantic Ocean

BAIE TERTIARY SHELL

BAIE GASPÉ

Strait of Belle Isle

WOODY POINT

WOODS ISLAND HARBOUR

Gulf of St.Lawrence

UNITED STATES

NEWPORT

NEWFOUNDLAND

TRINITY

ST. JOHN'S

IRELAND

ENGLAND

FRANCE

North Atlantic

I FIRST SAILED IN ATLANTIC ARCTIC WATERS, aboard *Belvedere*, on a passage from the Beaufort Sea to Sisimiut, Greenland. As we worked our way into Baffin Bay and headed toward Greenland, I began to comprehend how different things here were from what I had experienced for twenty years in the western Arctic. Instead of the West's relatively shallow waters, hemmed round by pack ice and the sandy continental shore, here were big seas, rolling across thousands of miles and full of heaving, bruised sea ice and icebergs driven by powerful weather systems and ocean currents. Moreover, the jagged coasts were mostly unforgiving hard rock cliffs and ledges, not the soft beaches and shoals that I had only recently left. I felt both menace and challenge. It was thrilling.

Faeringshavn

I left *Belvedere* in Sisimiut for the winter of 1988-1989, then took her down the west coast of Greenland before crossing the Labrador Sea, and on to New England. At Faeringshavn we began to get a feel for this ironbound coast.

Arsuk Fiord

On the southwest coast we stopped briefly at the Danish Naval base, Grønnedal. In this fiord, home to a few Norse settlers a thousand years ago, *Belvedere* is barely visible at the base of the cliff.

After refitting Belvedere *from the wear and tear of six winters in the Arctic, I crossed the Atlantic to Scotland in 1991. The following year we worked up the west coast of Scotland to Norway, via the Shetland Islands, and then on to Svalbard.*

Loch Tarbert, Isle of Jura, Scotland

We enjoyed the peacefulness of a June evening in the Western Isles.

On Mainland, Shetland

Lighthouse on the Coast of Norway

Arctic Circle,
Coast of Norway

As we passed the Arctic Circle monument on one of Norway's islands, the sky cleared, giving us a beautiful sunset.

Hornsund, Spitsbergen

In 1596 near Svalbard, Willem Barents discovered the large bowhead whale population of the Greenland Sea. His discovery set off an oil rush to its largest island, Spitsbergen. Both British and Dutch whalemen built stations at various spots on the island to process the whales' blubber and baleen. Here Norwegian archaeologists investigate the remains of a British whaling station of the early seventeenth century. Part of a bowhead's jaw is on the left.

Trapper's Camp, Bellsund, Spitsbergen

Polar bears are drawn to the smell of fat. On a morraine in Bellsund a Norwegian trapper set up a large tripod near his camp to store his meat supplies away from marauding bears.

Smeerenburg, Amsterdamøya, Spitsbergen

On an island off the northwest corner of Spitsbergen, at nearly 80 degrees North Latitude, the seventeenth-century Dutch whaling settlement of Smeerenburg ("Blubbertown") was probably the nothernmost large habitation on earth. Today little remains, but archaeologists have unearthed tryworks and well-preserved graves there. The shores are littered with driftwood from the Siberian rivers.

Danskøya, Spitsbergen

In the first half of the twentieth century, during the heyday of the fur trade, Norwegian trappers moved to the Svalbard archipelago. The remains of their camps are a reminder of their self-reliance and of the hardships they endured. Here, Bonnie Hahn examines a windlass at one of the abandoned camps.

The Faeroe Islands lie between Shetland and Iceland. In the eighth century A.D. the islands were colonized by Irish monks, who were driven away a hundred years later by Norse immigrants.

In 1993 I returned to North America via a route some Norsemen may have taken: the Outer Hebrides, Faeroe Islands, Iceland and Newfoundland. I had hoped to visit Greenland as well, but a thick band of drift ice on its shores denied us entrance, requiring instead a 1,200-mile run from Keflavik, Iceland to St. Anthony, Newfoundland.

Passage near Store Dimon, Faeroe Islands

The tidal currents in the Faeroes can run as fast as eight knots amid the bold green-topped islands.

Westmanna, Streymoy, Faeroe Islands

Turf is used as an effective insulation in the Nordic countries.

Southeast Coast of Iceland

Because there are very few harbors on the south coast of
Iceland, it must be treated with caution by mariners. It is
as unforgiving as it looks.

Interior Iceland

Iceland sits atop the Mid-Atlantic Ridge, and is being split apart by crustal movement. Iceland's interior valleys show the volcanic topography of the island. Sheep dot the fields as clouds dapple the landscape.

Gulf of Saint Lawrence, Newfoundland and Labrador

In 1995 I began a series of voyages on the coasts of the Gulf of Saint Lawrence, Newfoundland and Labrador, waters where Europeans have been fishing, and occasionally fighting, for five hundred years.

Newport, New Brunswick, Gulf of Saint Lawrence

In the shelter of Newport's harbor a thunderstorm swept over us.

Cape Gaspé, Quebec, Gulf of Saint Lawrence

As we entered Baie Gaspé a squall line crossed the bay.

Baie Tertiary Shell, Quebec-Labrador, Gulf of Saint Lawrence

Under a flaming sky we savored a quiet sunset on the coast of Quebec-Labrador in a bay that, I assume, can only have been named by a zealous geologist.

Cape Spear, Newfoundland

Cape Spear is the easternmost point in Newfoundland, hence North America. There we passed a large iceberg on the way in to St. John's Harbour. The next day, from the heights above the harbor entrance, the berg was still visible, drifting slowly south toward the Grand Banks.

Trinity, Newfoundland

On our way to Trinity, one of the oldest English settlements in Newfoundland, we traveled with a dramatic afternoon sky.

Woods Island Harbour, Bay of Islands, Newfoundland

Newfoundland's west coast springs into lush greenery in the sheltered bays, away from the Gulf of Saint Lawrence's winds.

Woody Point,
Bonne Bay,
Newfoundland

Cribwork docks built out over the water have served generations of Newfoundland's fishermen in this beautiful harbor. As one of the fishermen said to me about our mooring, "Yer as safe 'ere as if yer in God's pocket."

Iceberg, Strait of Belle Isle

Most icebergs are carried down the east coast of Newfoundland. A few, however, enter the Strait of Belle Isle, where they quickly melt in the warmer waters of the Gulf of Saint Lawrence. Icebergs continually shed small pieces of ice. Here we collect some to replenish *Belvedere*'s ice supply.

Red Bay, Labrador

Red Bay and several other harbors near the Strait of Belle Isle were the center of European commercial whaling in the early years of the sixteenth century. Basque whalemen set up stations on the Labrador shore to capture bowhead and right whales and render their blubber into oil. Today this quiet town has the northernmost vegetable gardens on the Labrador coast. Potatoes are grown in mounds, and the gardens are surrounded with cow parsley to cut the force of the wind.

The wreck of a collier off
Saddle Island is a reminder
of the strength of the
autumn winds in the Strait
of Belle Isle. Fog, too, is a
frequent summer visitor.

Chateau Bay, Labrador

A great basalt mesa gives Chateau Bay its name. Like nearby Red Bay, Chateau Bay was a Basque whaling port in the sixteenth century, but later it became a valuable fishing harbor for the English. Its strategic location at the north end of the Strait of Belle Isle caused the British to place a garrison of soldiers there during the wars of the mid-eighteenth century. Now it serves only as a summer outport for the fishermen and their families.

Battle Harbour, Labrador

Battle Harbour was settled by the English in 1775 when a trading company set up shop on the harbor's granite ledges. A village thrived there as a base for the cod and seal fisheries, but as the twentieth century wore on, the fisheries dwindled and the inhabitants slowly moved elsewhere. Today, the village has been restored as a living monument to the life and work of the Labradoreans of the last three centuries.

Battle Harbour is on "Iceberg Alley," the place where the cold, south-flowing Labrador Current passes closest to shore. Every year it carries more than a thousand icebergs past Battle Harbour.

Penney Harbour, Labrador

Penney Harbour's hard rock ledges provide excellent protection from the Labrador Sea's wind, swell and ice. As one Labradorean told me, "Go'in there, it's just like shuttin' the door."

Indian Tickle, Labrador

Indian Tickle is another of Labrador's abandoned fishing ports. In Labradorean parlance a "tickle" is a passage so narrow that the bushes on shore will tickle the sides of your boat.

Porcupine Strand, Labrador

The strand at Cape Porcupine is surely one of the most surprising sights in all of Labrador. Instead of bold granite headlands, here are twenty miles of sand beaches. Porcupine Strand appears in a Norse saga about a voyage to North America: the strands are identified as "Fudurstrandir"—"Marvel Strands."

Hawke Harbour, Labrador

At the head of Hawke Harbour lies a mass of wreckage: rusty tanks, smokestacks, conveyor belts, boilers and twisted metal rails. These are the remains of the Hawke Harbour whaling station, a processing plant that operated on and off, depending on market conditions, from 1905 until its fiery destruction in 1959.

Arctic Mirage, Cape Harrison to Cape Makkovik, Labrador

On the central Labrador coast, Capes Harrison, Makkovik and Harrigan jut out into the Labrador Sea like large hooks, snagging the ice flowing south in the Labrador Current. For the mariner, progress often requires zigzaging amid the floes, but when a northwesterly wind blows, putting warm air over the

cold water, the result is a mirage that distorts the floes vertically, giving the appearance of a solid wall of ice ahead. This is the famous "arctic mirage," a phenomenon that has fascinated writers and artists for centuries.

West Turnavik Island, Labrador

North of Cape Harrison, West Turnavik Island's tiny harbor gives refuge amid the outer islands. When a westerly wind dies in the evening, the result is a vivid sunset.

Hopedale, Labrador

The village of Hopedale was founded by the Moravian brethren of Germany in the eighteenth century. Athough the harbor is protected by outlying islands, it is vulnerable to drift ice driven by easterly winds. In 1996 I saw the ice moving toward the village, and, not wanting to be trapped there, we headed south quickly. Still, it took us a week of twisting and turning amid the floes to reach Cape Harrison and clear water (see pages 107–108).

The Inside Passage to Nain, Labrador

When it is blowing from the east, fog and rain frequent
the Labrador coast. It is possible to travel in the lee of the
outer islands, but the fog overtakes everything.

Man O'War Brook, Port Manvers Run, Labrador

Man O'War Brook cascades to Port Manvers Run in braided skeins. Here, with *Belvedere*'s stern warped in close to the brook's outfall, we are using a small electric pump and a garden hose to fill her water tanks.

The Bishop's Mitre, Cape Mugford, Labrador

The inside passage on the north Labrador coast ends at Cape Mugford and The Bishop's Mitre. Beyond, the sea breaks directly against the massive granite cliffs. Here, with a line of snow highlighting its crevice, the twin tops of the bishop's hat are partially obscured by clouds.

Hebron, Labrador

Silence envelops Hebron's empty buildings. Moravian brethren lived and worked here from 1837 to 1959, when the town was abandoned and the inhabitants moved to Nain. Decay and deterioration are everywhere: On the long dormitory-like building that housed both a small chapel and the missionaries themselves, the wind has torn the metal off the roof in places, collapsed the entryway housings, and damaged the weather vane atop its delicate cupola.

Ramah, Labrador

Like Hebron, Ramah was the site of a Moravian mission to the Inuit. Now nothing remains, save a small graveyard and the outlines where a few Inuit houses stood. We anchored off Ramah in a thick fog that lifted briefly to reveal the majesty of the fiord's 3,800-foot mountains.

Bear's Gut, Labrador

The headlands at the mouth of Bear's Gut present a forbidding appearance as layers of low clouds streak their cliffs.

Cape White Handkerchief, Labrador

Rising from the ocean in a 700-mile procession of granite shoals, islands, cliffs and mountains, Labrador's coast runs from the scrub-covered islets of Quebec to the jagged mountains in the north. Here, at Cape White Handkerchief, Labrador's Torngat Mountains form a bold palisade that comprises some of the oldest rocks on earth.

Afterword

THAT EVENING AT JABBERTOWN, nearly thirty years ago, I walked slowly back to our camp and rejoined the rhythm of the Eskimos' lives. It struck me then that, without realizing it, I had already been embarked on a voyage of discovery for ten years, and simultaneously I understood that I could not foretell its destination, nor did I wish to know where it would ultimately lead, because the voyage was so thoroughly enjoyable. To date this voyage has taken me more than 50,000 miles in boats in the North. It is a voyage begun, but not ended, I am glad to say.

Acknowledgments

MANY PERSONS HAVE BEEN EXTRAORDINARILY kind and helpful to me in my northern work. I cannot name them all, but I am most sincerely grateful to every one.

First I want to thank the more than 150 men and women with whom I have sailed throughout the North in my umiak, in *Belvedere*, in *Itasca*, and in many small boats. Others deserve special mention: Jim and Susie Andersen, Doug Anderson, Walt Audi, Jerry Austin, Hans-Georg Bandi, Christopher and Jackie Barlow, Bill Barr, Jim Bodena, Waldo Bodfish, Steve Braund, Lawson Brigham, Willard Brooks, Tom Brower, Lloyd Bugden, Randy Cahill, Hamilton Carter, Alan Cooke, Tom Crowley, Herb Davis, Dick Finnie, Henry and Susanna Fuller, Craig George, Carl Grauvogel, Bill Graves, Elmer Groth, Kavik Hahn, Ken Hahn, Pat Hahn, Jim Hamblin, George Hobson, Jim Houston, Father Leonce d'Hurtevant,

Carl Jewell, Sven Johansson, Allan Jouning, the Laurie Kingik family, the Luke Koonook family, Willy Laserich, Molly Lee, Father Robert Lemeur, John Lennie, Ernie Lyall, Malcolm and Anne MacGregor, Elizabeth Mackenzie, Father Guy Mary-Rouselliere, Dwight and Jesse Milligrock, Lionel Montpetit, Edmund and Darlene Moores, Richard K. Nelson, Cornelius Osgood, Tom Padden, Charlie Pedersen, Ted Pedersen, Carl Emil Peterson, George Washington Porter, Sr., George and Effie Porter, Paul Preville, Tom Pullen, Froelich Rainey, Tom Robinson, Andy Rowe, Graham and Diana Rowley, Blayney Scott, David Scott Cowper, Peter and Alma Semotiuk, Leon Shelabarger, Newbold Smith, Nick Smith, Benny Souyri, Jem and Maur Tetley, Douglas Thomas, Ray Tomsett, Patrick Toomey, Glenn and Trish Warner, Link and Tahoe Washburn, William E. Simon, who invited me to participate in his Northwest Passage traverse aboard *Itasca*, Nick Whitman, who encouraged me to produce this book, and John Thornton, who steered it to completion.

Lastly I want to thank Bonnie Hahn, to whom this book is dedicated, for her constant support of, and participation in, my projects. This book would not have been possible without her help.